Little Giant Papa Ge

Written by Papa's granddaughter
Elana Gelman Roumell

Illustrated by TVT Art Teacher (2001-2018)
Helaine Yeskel

Edited by Elana's Ema (Mother)
Bernice Tabak Kirzner

In Memory of
Irving "Papa" Gelman

January 24, 1925 to March 4, 2018
28 Tevet 5685   17 Adar 5778

May your legacy remain in the hearts and souls
of our future generations.

Irving "Papa" Gelman

Irving "Papa" Gelman was born in Hosht, Poland and survived the Holocaust by hiding under a barn for 16 months. In April 1947, Gelman immigrated to New York City with a total of $5.60. He promptly sent Rochelle, his soon-to-be wife, a telegram confirming he was waiting for her. Gelman began working in a textile business for $35 a week. Seven years later, he established his own textile company named Domka Inc., after the Ukrainian woman who saved his life by hiding him and his family on her farm.

"The key to Jewish culture is teaching." Irving Gelman

Gelman's commitment to Jewish education began with his father who was involved in starting a school in Poland designed to promote Jewish culture and survival. The school was called Tarbut, which means "culture". Gelman's passion for Jewish education led him to help manage and secure funding for two Jewish schools in New Jersey, Yavneh Academy and The Frisch School, before relocating to Orange County in 1984.

In 1991, Gelman founded Tarbut V'Torah (TVT) Community Day School, in loving memory of his daughter, Naomi Gelman Weiss. Since opening, TVT has grown from 36 students to a flourishing TK-12 college preparatory school with nearly 700 students at its height, making it one of the largest Jewish Day Schools in the nation.

The thousands of students who have attended TVT looked forward to being greeted by "Papa" Gelman whose big hugs, warm heart, keen mind and boundless energy had guided the school to remarkable success. In the process of building a school for our children, "Papa" Gelman had built a community committed to Jewish learning and living.

Papa Gelman with his first great grandchild, Noah Joshua Robles

A note from the author...

In the middle of the night before my Papa's memorial service and funeral, I woke with challenging questions. "How will I teach my children what a special man Papa was? How will I keep Papa's legacy alive in our future generations now that he is gone?"

It is all too easy to get wrapped up in our day-to-day routines. Weeks, months and years fly by so quickly. Before we know it, our loved ones who have passed are remembered only on their yahrzeit (anniversary of their passing) as our busy lives goes on. But, Papa's memory is far too significant to allow this to happen.

So, I woke in the middle of the night with a vision. I will write a story about Papa and read it to my own children every night so his legacy is never forgotten and his character remains alive in the minds and hearts of those who read his book!

Papa with the author's first child, Aviva Dahlia, who was the inspiration for writing this story.

The words just came to me. The lines kept on emerging. By dawn I had the story complete and my devastating thoughts of his lost memory transformed into faith that his legacy will remain. I thought, "My kids now will always know of the great man Papa Gelman was!"

I went back to sleep and woke the next day to attend Papa's memorial service and funeral. I had the honor of reading this story aloud to the thousand people in attendance. I was mobbed by parents requesting that I publish this story so they too could also read it to their children.

So here it is. *Little Giant Papa Gelman* is now available for all who wish to keep Papa's memory alive and continue teaching generation after generation about the great man Papa Gelman was.

'd like to acknowledge each of Papa's grandkids, my siblings and cousins, who each in their own way also share a piece of Papa with the world.

Rebecca Duel
Lonny Weiss
Leora Gelman Robles
Elana Gelman Roumell
Lavy Weiss
Joshua Gelman z"l
Lyla Weiss
L Jacob Weiss

We have shared our Papa with thousands of others our entire lives. On behalf of my family, we thank you for continuing to share our Papa with your children, grandchildren, and future generations.

With love,

Elana Gelman Roumell

Papa with granddaughter and author,
Elana Gelman Roumell

There once lived a little giant,
who made a BIG difference in the world.

He walked around with candies,
passed them out to boys and girls.

He was a cute little man,
short in stature with a friendly grin.

Although a little man, he had a GIANT heart like
no one there's ever been.

Little giant Papa has cried many, many tears.

But kept on living life without any fears.

After surviving a horrible war.

And tragically losing his daughter Naomi,
son Glenn and grandson Joshie

You would think he couldn't take it anymore!

But that didn't stop your Papa from doing
more... more ...and more.

Little giant Papa wiped his tears away.

And chose to turn his tears into purpose and passion, illuminating the way.

He loved Jewish life, and was committed to his Shul.

So one day he decided to start another school.

He worked through his heart.
Never giving up on his vision.

For our little giant Papa was on a special mission.

He helped teach thousands of kids, just like you,
about Jewish culture and Torah.
And named his school, Tarbut V' Torah.

He wants you to know you can accomplish anything. As long as you give to others and are grateful for everything.

Little giant Papa is with you every day.
When you're ever in need just ask him and he'll say,

"Bubbale, I love you with all my heart.
Now go do good things in the world and know we are
never apart."

The End

May Papa Gelman's spirit
survive in the hearts of us all.
May his legacy be an inspiration to do Tikkun Olam
as we continue to heal the world.

If you enjoyed this book,
please consider gifting one to
another family that you think can also be inspired
by Papa Gelman's story.

Proceeds from the sale of this book
will go to support Jewish causes.

Made in the USA
Middletown, DE
14 April 2022

64250124R00015